Here's all the great literature in this grade level of *Celebrate Reading!*

BOOK A

Once Upon a Hippo

Ways of Telling Stories

Hot Hippo
by Mwenye Hadithi
Illustrations by
Adrienne Kennaway
✳ KATE GREENAWAY
AUTHOR/ILLUSTRATOR MEDAL

Rosa and Blanca
retold by Joe Hayes
Illustrations by José Ortega

Featured Poets

Beatrice Schenk de Regniers
Ed Young

BOOK B

The Big Blank Piece of Paper

Artists at Work

BOOK C

You Be the Bread and I'll Be the Cheese

Showing How We Care

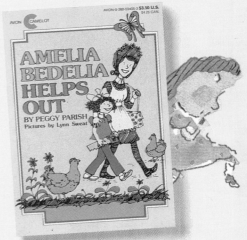

The Relatives Came
Story by CYNTHIA RYLANT illustrated by STEPHEN GAMMELL

Featured Poets

Mary Ann Hoberman
Charlotte Pomerantz

BOOK D

Why Does Water Wiggle?

Learning About the World

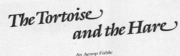

Featured Poets

Jack Prelutsky
Lessie Jones Little

BOOK E

How to Talk to Bears

And Other Tips for Success

BOOK F

Bathtub Voyages

Tales of Adventure

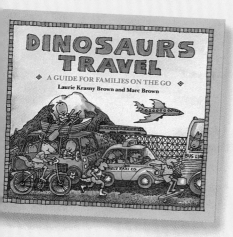

Featured Poets

John Ciardi
Sioux Indian Songs

Celebrate Reading!
Trade Book Library

Frog and Toad Together
by Arnold Lobel
✳ NEWBERY MEDAL HONOR BOOK
✳ ALA NOTABLE CHILDREN'S BOOK
✳ *SCHOOL LIBRARY JOURNAL* BEST BOOK
✳ READING RAINBOW SELECTION
✳ LIBRARY OF CONGRESS
CHILDREN'S BOOK

**The Lady with the
Alligator Purse**
by Nadine Bernard Westcott
✳ CHILDREN'S CHOICE

**Henry and Mudge in
Puddle Trouble**
by Cynthia Rylant
✳ GARDEN STATE CHILDREN'S
BOOK AWARD

Tyrannosaurus Was a Beast
by Jack Prelutsky
✳ OUTSTANDING SCIENCE TRADE BOOK

A Chair for My Mother
by Vera Williams
✳ CALDECOTT MEDAL HONOR BOOK
✳ ALA NOTABLE CHILDREN'S BOOK
✳ READING RAINBOW SELECTION
✳ BOSTON GLOBE-HORN BOOK AWARD

Paul Bunyan
by Steven Kellogg
✳ READING RAINBOW SELECTION

Big & Little Book Library

Rockabye Crocodile
by Jose Aruego and
Ariane Dewey

Putting on a Play
by Caroline Feller Bauer
Illustrations by Cyd Moore
✳ CHRISTOPHER AWARD AUTHOR

We Are Best Friends
by Aliki
✳ CHILDREN'S CHOICE AUTHOR

Fables from Around the World
retold by Lily Toy Hong,
Carmen Tafolla, Tom Paxton,
Joseph Bruchac, and
Nancy Ross Ryan

Wings: A Tale of Two Chickens
by James Marshall
✳ CHILDREN'S CHOICE AUTHOR
✳ PARENTS' CHOICE AUTHOR
✳ ALA NOTABLE BOOK AUTHOR

Is There Life in Outer Space?
by Franklyn M. Branley
Illustrations by Don Madden
✳ READING RAINBOW BOOK

Once Upon a Hippo

Ways
of Telling
Stories

Titles in This Set

Once Upon a Hippo

The Big Blank Piece of Paper

You Be the Bread and I'll Be the Cheese

Why Does Water Wiggle?

How to Talk to Bears

Bathtub Voyages

About the Cover Artist
Etienne Delessert is from Switzerland, but he now lives in
Connecticut. His dog's name is Yak. He has written and
illustrated many books for children.

ISBN 0-673-82088-2

1995 printing
Copyright © 1993
Scott, Foresman and Company, Glenview, Illinois
All Rights Reserved.
Printed in the United States of America.

Acknowledgments appear on page 128.

12345678910VHJ999897969594

Once Upon a Hippo

Ways of Telling Stories

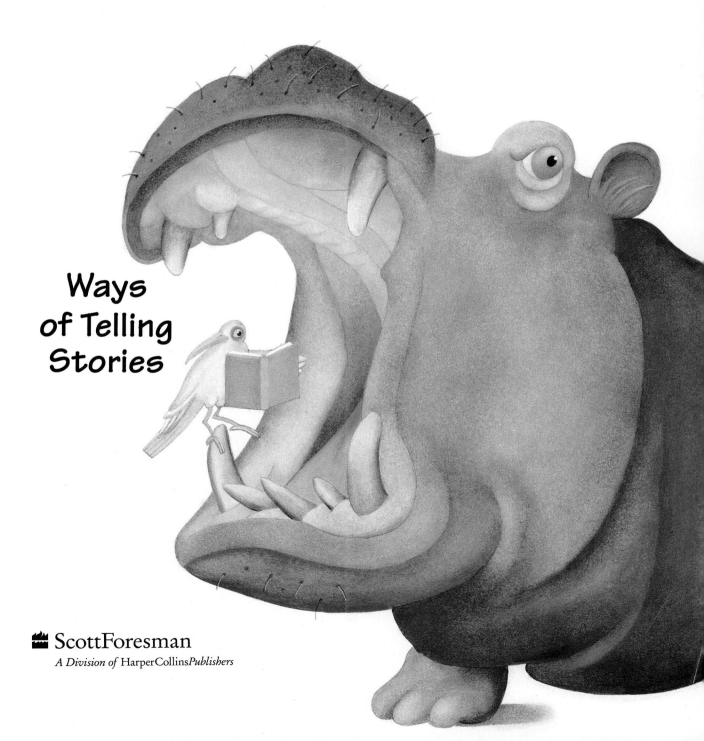

ScottForesman

A Division of HarperCollinsPublishers

Contents

Tell Me a Tale!

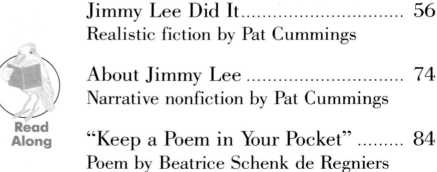

The Words and Pictures of Pat Cummings
Author Study

Read Along

Folk Tale Fun
Genre Study

Student Resources

THREE UP A TREE

by James Marshall

"Wow!" said Spider. "Will you look at *that*!"

Some big kids down the street had built a swell tree house.

"Can we come up?" called out Sam.

"No!" said the big kids.

"Well!" said Spider.

"Never mind," said Sam. "We'll build our own tree house."

"Let's ask Lolly to help," said Spider.

But Lolly would not help. "I'm too busy," she said.

"You call *that* busy?" said Spider.

"Let's go," said Sam.

In no time Spider and Sam were as busy as squirrels. Meanwhile Lolly decided to take a little snooze.

When Lolly woke up the tree house was finished.

"Wow," she said. "I'll be right up."

"Oh, no," said Sam. "You didn't help."

"Oh, *please,*" said Lolly.

"No!" said Spider.

"I know some good stories," said Lolly.

"Stories?" said Sam. "I love a
good story."

Lolly was up the tree in a flash.
"Now tell us a story," said Sam.
"And make it good," said Spider.
"Sit down," said Lolly. "And listen
to this."

Lolly's Story

One summer evening a doll and a chicken went for a walk. And they got lost.

"Oh, no," said the doll.

Just then a monster came around the corner.

"Oh, no," said the doll.

"Let's run!" cried the chicken.

And they ran as fast as they could.

"He's right behind us!" cried
the chicken.

"Oh, no!" said the doll.

"Quick!" cried the chicken. "Let's
climb that tree!"

And they did—in a jiffy. But
monsters know how to climb trees too.
   "He's got us now!" cried the
chicken.
   "Oh, no!" cried the doll.
   The monster opened his mouth.

"Will you tie my new shoes?"
he said.

"Oh, yes!" said the doll.

"Not much of a story," said Spider.
"The end was too sweet."
"Can you tell a better story?"
said Lolly.
"Listen to this," said Spider.

Spider's Story

A chicken caught the wrong bus. She found herself in a bad part of town—the part of town where foxes live.

"Uh-oh," she said.

Quickly she pulled down her hat and waited for the next bus. But very soon—you guessed it—a hungry fox came along and sat beside her.

His eyes were not good. But there was nothing wrong with his nose.

"I can smell that you're having chicken tonight," he said.

"Er . . ." said the chicken. "Yes, I have just been to the store."

"I *love* chicken," said the fox. "How will you cook it?"

The chicken knew she had to be clever. She did not want the fox to invite himself to dinner.

"Well," she said. "I always cook my chicken in sour chocolate milk with lots of pickles and rotten eggs."

"It sounds delicious," said the fox. "May I come to dinner?"

"Let's see," said the chicken. "That will make ten of us."

Well, *that* was too many for the fox!

He grabbed the chicken's grocery
bag and ran away.

"All for me!" he cried. "All
for me!"

The poor chicken flew up into a
nearby tree to wait for the next bus.
(She should have done that in the
first place.)

P.S. When the fox got home, he
reached into the bag. But there
was no chicken inside. Only the
chicken's favorite food. Can you guess
what it was?

"Worms!" cried Lolly. "Worms!
That story wasn't bad."

"Not bad at all," said Sam. "But
now it's *my* turn."

Sam's Story

A monster woke up from a nap. He was *very* hungry.

"I want ice cream," he said. "Lots of it."

He went out to buy some. But he got lost.

"Oh, well," he said. "I'll just ask someone for help."

At that moment a fox came around
the corner.

"Excuse me," said the monster.

"Help!" cried the fox. "I'm getting
out of here!"

And away he went.

"How rude," said the monster.

He put on the fox's hat, scarf,
and glasses.

Just then a doll and a chicken came
around the corner.

"Hi," said the chicken.

"Will you help me find some ice
cream?" said the monster.

"If you will give us a ride in your
wagon," said the chicken.

And off they went.

"Stop!" said the chicken. "This is the place for ice cream."

"Oh really?" said the monster.

"Wait here," said the doll. "We'll be right back."

In a moment they were back.

"Step on it!" said the doll. "You
don't want your ice cream to melt!"

"I'll hurry!" said the monster.

"Faster!" cried the chicken.

The monster ran as fast as he could.
Soon they came to a big tree.

"This is where we live," said the
doll.

And they all climbed up the tree.
The doll and the chicken opened their
bags. But there was no ice cream
inside. There was only money.

"Oh, no!" said the monster. "You are
bank robbers!"

The monster took off his hat, scarf, and glasses. The doll and the chicken were scared out of their wits.

"Help, help!" they cried. "Let's get out of here!"

And they ran as fast as their little legs could carry them.

The monster returned the money to
the bank. As a reward he was given all
the ice cream he could eat. And there
was *lots* of it!

"My story was better," said Lolly.

"No, mine was," said Spider.

"No, mine!" said Sam.

"Let's hear them again," said Lolly.
  And they did.

Thinking About It

1. Did Lolly, Spider, or Sam surprise you? Scare you? Make you laugh? Tell about it.

2. "Mine's the best!" That's how Spider, Sam, and Lolly all feel about their own stories. Which story do you think was the best? Tell what made it a good story.

3. Lolly, Sam, and Spider have invited you up to their tree house to tell a story. Make up another story about the doll, the chicken, the monster, and the fox.

Another Book by James Marshall

Lolly, Sam, and Spider are back for some splashy adventures in *Three By the Sea.*

There's a Hole in the Bucket

pictures by Nadine Bernard Westcott

There's a hole in the bucket, dear Liza, dear Liza,
There's a hole in the bucket, dear Liza, a hole.

Well, fix it, dear Henry, dear Henry, dear Henry,
Well, fix it, dear Henry, dear Henry, fix it.

With what shall I fix it, dear Liza, dear Liza,
With what shall I fix it, dear Liza, with what?

With a straw, dear Henry, dear Henry, dear Henry,
With a straw, dear Henry, dear Henry, with a straw.

But the straw is too long, dear Liza, dear Liza,
But the straw is too long, dear Liza, too long.

Then cut it, dear Henry, dear Henry, dear Henry,
Then cut it, dear Henry, dear Henry, then cut it.

Well, how shall I cut it, dear Liza, dear Liza,
Well, how shall I cut it, dear Liza, well how?

With an axe, dear Henry, dear Henry, dear Henry,
With an axe, dear Henry, dear Henry, with an axe.

But the axe is too dull, dear Liza, dear Liza,
But the axe is too dull, dear Liza, too dull.

Then sharpen it, dear Henry, dear Henry, dear Henry,
Then sharpen it, dear Henry, dear Henry, then sharpen it.

On what shall I sharpen it, dear Liza, dear Liza,
On what shall I sharpen it, dear Liza, on what?

On a stone, dear Henry, dear Henry, dear Henry,
On a stone, dear Henry, dear Henry, on a stone.

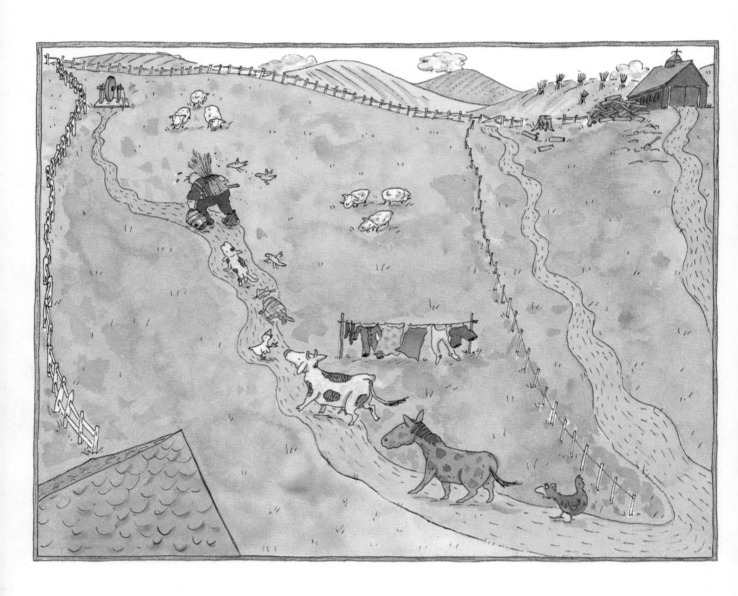

But the stone is too dry, dear Liza, dear Liza,
But the stone is too dry, dear Liza, too dry.

Then wet it, dear Henry, dear Henry, dear Henry,
Then wet it, dear Henry, dear Henry, then wet it.

With what shall I wet it, dear Liza, dear Liza,
With what shall I wet it, dear Liza, with what?

With water, dear Henry, dear Henry, dear Henry,
With water, dear Henry, dear Henry, with water.

Well, how shall I carry it, dear Liza, dear Liza,
Well, how shall I carry it, dear Liza, well how?

In a bucket, dear Henry, dear Henry, dear Henry,
In a bucket, dear Henry, dear Henry, in a bucket.

BUT THERE'S A HOLE IN THE BUCKET,
DEAR LIZA, DEAR LIZA,
THERE'S A HOLE IN THE BUCKET,
DEAR LIZA, A HOLE.

Traditional
arr. Ray Kimmelman

There's a hole in the buck-et, dear Li-za, dear
Well __ fix it, dear __ Hen-ry, dear Hen-ry, dear

Li - za, there's a hole in the buck-et, dear Li-za, a hole.
Hen - ry, well __ fix it, dear __ Hen-ry, dear Hen-ry, fix it.

50

Thinking About It

1. Look at all the pictures. Which picture would you like to step into? While you are there, how will you help?

2. Liza and Henry are working in their house and yard. Who do you think works harder? Tell why.

3. Oh, no! The bucket can't be fixed! What else can you do with a bucket that has a hole in it?

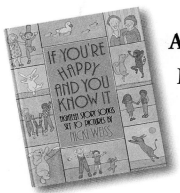

Another Book of Songs

Music time! You'll find story songs from around the world in *If You're Happy and You Know It,* illustrated by Nicki Weiss.

Two Chinese Rhymes

pictures by
Ed Young

高高山上一顆蘇有個吉了兒往上爬

我問吉了兒你上那他說渴了要吃蘇

On the top of a mountain
A grass blade was growing,
And up it a cricket was busily climbing.
I said to him, "Cricket,
Now where are you going?"
He answered me loudly, "I'm going out dining!"

四個蹄子分八瓣腦袋長在脖子上

There's a cow on the mountain,
The old saying goes;
At the end of her legs
Are four feet and eight toes.
Her tail hangs behind
At the end of her back,
And her head sticks out front
At the end of her neck.

高高山上一個牛尾巴長在屁股後

53

Crickets Are More Than Bugs!

by Ed Young

Ed Young

I painted the pictures for the two Chinese rhymes you read. I am from China, and Chinese children have always loved to sing rhymes like these.

Many Chinese rhymes are about things children enjoy, like crickets. To Chinese people, crickets are more than creepy crawly bugs. They are pets! But crickets have short lives. They only live one summer.

I had many cricket pets when I was a young boy. When fall came, I tried to keep my crickets alive. I made silk-lined matchboxes for them and kept them in a warm place. But my crickets would still die. I was sad each fall, but every summer I found new crickets for pets.

Now that you know about crickets, I hope you can see why they are more than bugs!

杨志成

JIMMY LEE
DID IT

by Pat Cummings

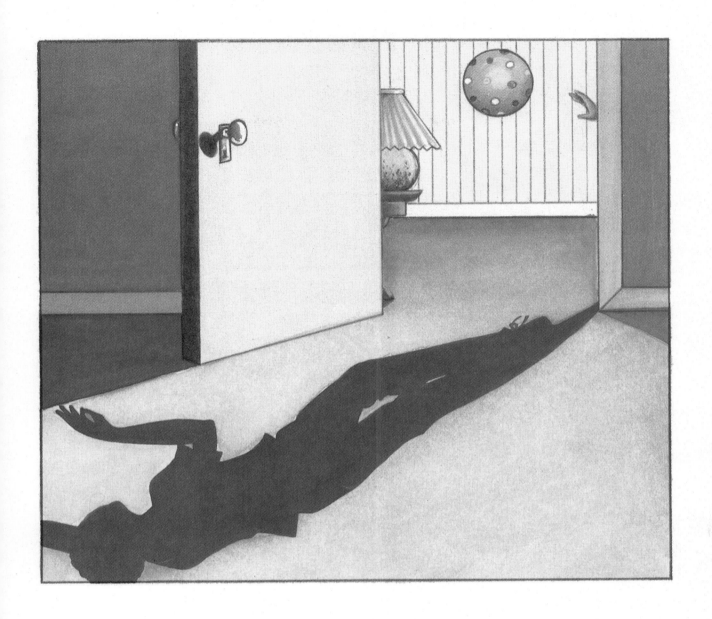

Jimmy Lee is back again
And nothing is the same.

He's causing lots of trouble,
While my brother takes the blame.

Artie made his bed, he said.

But Jimmy thinks he's smart.

While Artie read his comics,
Jimmy pulled the sheets apart.

Dad fixed us pancakes
And Artie said his tasted fine,

But Jimmy Lee had just been there
And eaten most of mine.

I heard the crash of breaking glass,
    But turned too late, I guess.

"Jimmy Lee did it," Artie said,
    As we cleaned up the mess.

When Artie's room got painted,
Jimmy Lee was in the hall.

He used up Artie's crayons
Drawing pictures on the wall.

And when I finally found my bear,
I asked Artie, "Who hid it?"

He told me frankly, "Angel,
It was Jimmy Lee who did it."

He caused so much trouble
That I began to see—

The only way to stop it
Was to capture Jimmy Lee.

I knew about his sweet tooth,
So I set a tasty trap,

But Jimmy Lee just waited
Till I had to take my nap.

I spread out all my marbles
To trip up Jimmy Lee.

The dog slid by and scratched the floor
And Mom got mad at me.

I hid in the hall closet
And I never made a sound,

But Jimmy Lee will only come
When Artie is around.

I don't know what he looks like,

He never leaves a trace—

Except for spills and tears
And Artie's things about the place.

Since Artie won't describe him,
He remains a mystery.

But if you're smart, you'll listen
And watch out for Jimmy Lee.

THINKING ABOUT IT

1. If you could see Jimmy Lee, what would you say to him? How would you feel if Jimmy Lee lived in your house? Tell why you would feel that way.

2. Angel tried hard to catch Jimmy Lee. Why couldn't she catch him? How would you try to catch him?

3. Jimmy Lee has come to your classroom! What's going to happen now?

ABOUT JIMMY LEE

by Pat Cummings

Jimmy Lee Did It is a true story. My brother, Artie, had an imaginary friend named Jimmy Lee. Nobody else ever saw or heard Jimmy Lee. But Jimmy Lee made me crazy! I never knew where he was or what he would mess up next.

I really wrote the story to get back at Artie for all the things he blamed on Jimmy Lee. My younger sister, Barbara, was nicknamed Angel. In the story, she tries to find Jimmy Lee. Since I never knew what Jimmy Lee looked like, you never see him in the book. And since I have had to guess about who he was, I wanted anyone who read the story to have to guess, too. I even put clues in the pictures!

Here are the real Angel and Artie, along with me on the right.

I worked on writing the story until I was happy with it. Then, I started sketching. Sketching is like thinking on paper. I drew pictures of what might happen on each page. The pictures had to go with my words.

Next, I made my own dummy book—a handmade book with blank pages. A dummy book helps me plan where to put the words and pictures of my story. In my dummy book, I wrote the words and sketched each page. Sometimes, if I got a better idea, I made changes from my first sketches. Once I finished my plan, I was ready to draw the pictures.

I found a boy and girl who looked a lot like Artie and Angel did when they were little. I also found a dog, Kasper. Kasper lived downstairs from me.

I took photographs of Kasper and the children doing whatever the story showed them doing. I didn't always follow my dummy exactly. When Angel holds a teddy bear in the book, for example, the girl was really holding a pillow.

Then I looked at the photographs and drew outlines for each picture. If a nose or a hand didn't look right, I fixed it by tracing over it again with tracing paper. I did lots of erasing and moving things around until I got a drawing I was happy with. I traced the final outline onto watercolor paper. Then the fun began!

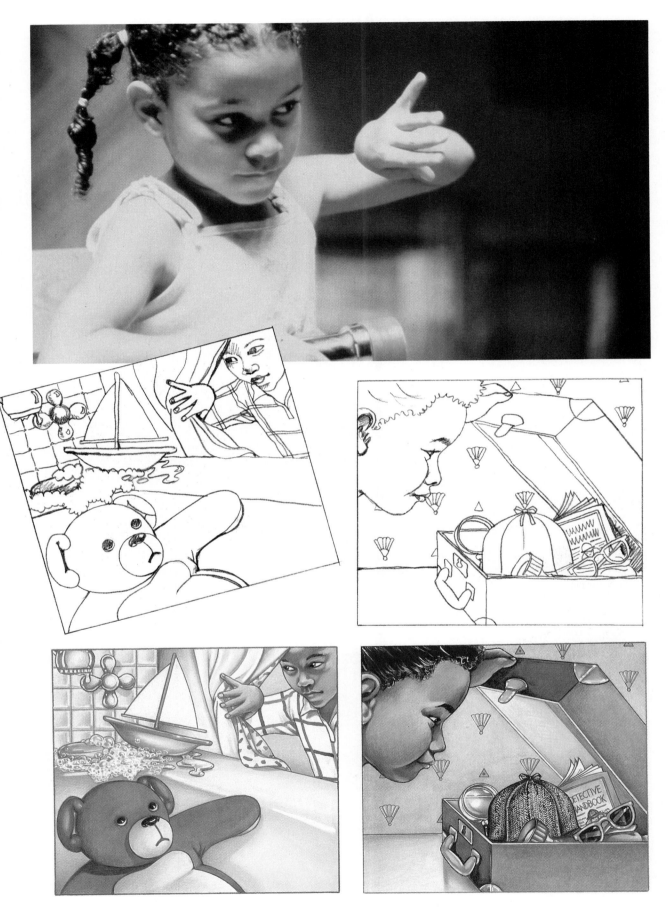

First, I painted everything with watercolors. Then, I used colored pencils to make the colors brighter in some places and softer in others. Next, I used pencils with fine points to outline everything in the drawings.

Finally, I used white paint to add little spots I wanted to be a crisp white . . . like a dot in the eye to make it shine. It took me over six months to paint all the pictures!

By the way, did you see the page in the story with the comics? When we were little, Artie used to tell me he was a superhero. He called himself the Crampo Kid. His superpower was that he could put cramps in his toes whenever he wanted!

When I wrote *Jimmy Lee Did It*, I put in the Crampo Kid. When my brother Artie saw that, it made him crazy! But I finally got back at him for all the things that Jimmy Lee did when we were kids.

THINKING ABOUT IT

1. Pat Cummings likes to tell stories about things that happened when she was a child. What do you like to tell stories about?

2. If you met Pat Cummings, what would you like to ask her? Why?

3. Be an illustrator! Choose a story. How will you illustrate it? Why will you illustrate it that way?

Another Book by Pat Cummings
In *Clean Your Room, Harvey Moon!*, Harvey has a big cleaning job to do, but he doesn't want to miss his favorite cartoons!

Keep a Poem in Your Pocket

by Beatrice Schenk de Regniers
illustration by Pat Cummings

Keep a poem in your pocket
and a picture in your head
and you'll never feel lonely
at night when you're in bed.

The little poem will sing to you
the little picture bring to you
a dozen dreams to dance to you
at night when you're in bed.

So—
Keep a picture in your pocket
and a poem in your head
and you'll never feel lonely
at night when you're in bed.

HOT HIPPO

by Mwenye Hadithi   Illustrated by Adrienne Kennaway

Hippo was hot.

He sat on the river bank
and gazed at the little fishes
swimming in the water.

If only I could live in
the water, he thought, how
wonderful life would be.

So he walked and he ran and he strolled
and he hopped and he lumbered along until he
came to the mountain where Ngai lived.

Ngai was the god of
Everything and Everywhere.

91

Ngai told the animals to live
on the land and the fishes
to live in the sea.

Ngai told the birds to fly in the air
and the ants to live under the ground.

Ngai had told Hippo he was to live
on the land and eat grass.

"Please, O great Ngai, god of Everything and Everywhere, I would so much like to live in the rivers and streams," begged Hippo hopefully. "I would still eat grass."

"Aha!" thundered the voice of Ngai.
"So you say. But one day you might, just might, eat a fish to see if it tasted good. And then you would
EAT ALL MY LITTLE FISHES!"

"Oh no, I promise I wouldn't," said Hippo.

"Aha!" thundered the voice of Ngai.
"So you say! But how can I be sure of that? I LOVE MY LITTLE FISHES!"

"I would show you," promised Hippo.
"I will let you look in my mouth whenever you like, to see that I am not eating your little fishes.

"And I will stir up the water with
my tail so you can see I have not
hidden the bones."

"Aha!" thundered the voice of Ngai.
"Then you may live in the water but..."
Hippo waited...

"...But you must come out of the
water at night and eat grass, so that
even in the dark I can tell you are
not eating my little fishes. Agreed?"

"Agreed!" sang Hippo happily.

And he ran all the way home
until he got to the river,
where he jumped in with a
mighty SPLASH!

99

And he sank like a stone,
because he couldn't swim.

But he could hold his breath and run along the bottom, which he does to this very day.

And he stirs up the bottom by wagging his little tail, so that Ngai can see he has not hidden any fish-bones.

101

And now and then he floats to the top
and opens his huge mouth ever so wide
and says: "Look, Ngai! No fishes!"

THINKING ABOUT IT

1. Hippo wanted to live in the water more than anything else. What is something you have wanted more than anything else?

2. I am a fish. Something hot and hippo-looking is getting into my water. Quick! Tell me what to do!

3. *Hot Hippo* explains why hippos live in the water and open their mouths wide. Make up a story that explains something about your favorite animal.

Another Book by Mwenye Hadithi

In *Tricky Tortoise*, Tortoise says he can jump over Elephant's head. Is Tortoise tricky enough to do it?

Rosa and Blanca

by Joe Hayes
illustrated by José Ortega

Once there were two sisters named Rosa and Blanca. They loved each other very much. If their mother sent Rosa to the store to buy flour for tortillas, Blanca would go with her. If their mother told Blanca to sweep the sidewalk in front of their house, Rosa would help her.

Their mother would always say, "My daughters are so good to one another. They make me very happy. I think I am the luckiest mother in the town. No. I am the luckiest mother in the country. No. I am the luckiest mother in the whole world!"

When Rosa and Blanca grew up, Rosa got married. She and her husband had three children. Blanca didn't get married. She lived alone.

One year Rosa planted a garden. Blanca planted a garden, too. They planted corn and tomatoes and good hot *chiles*.

When the tomatoes were round and ripe, Rosa helped Blanca pick the tomatoes in her garden. Blanca helped Rosa pick the tomatoes in her garden.

That night Rosa thought, "My poor sister Blanca lives all alone. She has no one to help her make a living. I have a husband and helpful children. I will give her half of my tomatoes to sell in the market."

Rosa filled a basket with tomatoes. She started toward Blanca's house.

That very same night Blanca thought, "My poor sister Rosa has a husband and three children. There are five to feed in her house. I only have myself. I will give her half of my tomatoes to sell in the market."

Blanca filled a basket with tomatoes. She started toward Rosa's house. The night was dark. The two sisters did not see each other when they passed.

Rosa added her tomatoes to the pile in Blanca's kitchen. Blanca added her tomatoes to the pile in Rosa's kitchen.

The next day Rosa looked at her pile of tomatoes. "*¡Vaya!*" she said. "How can I have so many tomatoes? Did my tomatoes have babies during the night?"

The next day Blanca looked at her pile of tomatoes. "*¡Vaya!*" she said. "How can I have so many tomatoes? Did my tomatoes have babies during the night?"

When the corn was ripe, Rosa helped Blanca pick her corn. Blanca helped Rosa pick her corn.

That night Rosa thought, "I will give half of my corn to Blanca to sell in the market."

That night Blanca thought, "I will give half of my corn to Rosa to sell in the market."

Each sister filled a basket with corn. Rosa went to Blanca's house. Blanca went to Rosa's house. The night was dark. They did not see each other when they passed.

Rosa added her corn to the corn in Blanca's house. Blanca added her corn to the corn in Rosa's house.

The next day Rosa said, "¡*Vaya!* How can I have so much corn? Did each ear invite a friend to spend the night?"

The next day Blanca said, "¡*Vaya!* How can I have so much corn? Did each ear invite a friend to spend the night?"

When the *chiles* were red and hot, Rosa
helped Blanca pick her *chiles*. Blanca helped
Rosa pick her *chiles*.

That night Rosa thought, "I will give Blanca
half of my *chiles* to sell in the market."

That night Blanca thought, "I will give Rosa
half of my *chiles* to sell in the market."

Each sister filled a basket with *chiles*.

Just then Rosa's youngest child started to cry.
Rosa went to the child's room. She picked him
up and rocked him.

Blanca was on her way to Rosa's house.

When Rosa's child went to sleep, Rosa picked up her basket of *chiles*. She started out the door. Blanca was coming in the door.

They both said, "*¡Vaya!*"

Rosa said, "Blanca, what are you doing? Why do you have that basket of *chiles*?"

Blanca said, "Rosa, what are you doing? Why do you have that basket of *chiles*?"

Rosa said, "I was going to give half of my *chiles* to you."

Blanca said, "But I was going to give half of my *chiles* to you!" Both sisters laughed.

Rosa said, "So that is why I still had so many tomatoes!"

Blanca said, "So that is why I still had so much corn!" The sisters hugged each other.

The next day Rosa and Blanca went to their mother's house. They told their mother what they had done.

Their old mother smiled and hugged her daughters. She said, "My daughters are so good to one another. They make me very happy. I think I am the luckiest mother in the town. No. I am the luckiest mother in the country. No. I am the luckiest mother in the whole world!"

The Gift of a Story

by Joe Hayes

Joe Hayes

When I was a child, my dad shared something special with me—his stories. He told me about things that had happened when he was a boy. Sometimes he made up stories about giants or elves. I loved listening to him tell stories. He really made the giants roar!

When I grew up and had children of my own, I wanted to give them something special. I remembered how much I liked the stories my dad told me. I thought, "Many years ago parents told their children folk tales that they had heard from their own parents. I'll learn folk tales and tell them to my children."

Folk tales are good stories to tell. Long before anyone wrote them down in books, folk tales were told out loud. They were passed along from parents to children for hundreds and hundreds of years. Each teller had his or her own way of telling the story.

I started to learn folk tales. Some were from New Mexico, because that's where I live. Sometimes people told me folk tales, and sometimes I found them in books. I learned Indian stories and Hispanic folk tales. I learned the tales that cowboys told around their campfires. I told the folk tales to my children in my own words.

Kathleen and Adam, my children, liked some of the folk tales very much. They asked me to tell their favorite stories over and over. I would change the story a little each time I told it.

I liked telling folk tales so much I looked for more children to tell them to. I went to schools. The children in the schools liked folk tales, too. Once when I told children a story, a girl said to me, "You just gave me a dream!" That made me feel good. I like it when my stories make someone happy.

If you would like to have a special gift to give people, learn a folk tale. You can find folk tales in books. Teachers and librarians know folk tales. Maybe your parents will want to share a favorite folk tale. Learn what happens in the story. Tell it in your own words. You will be a storyteller!

Pulling the Theme Together

Sharing Stories

1. Do you want Rosa and Blanca to be your sisters? Why or why not? How would you want them to treat you? How would you treat them?

2. Which story in this book would you like to tell to someone else? Why did you choose that story? How would you make the story fun to hear?

3. Everyone in this book is going to the tree house with Sam, Spider, and Lolly for a storytelling party. Which character in this book would you like to be? Tell why. Then tell a story that your character would make up.

127

Books to Enjoy

All of Our Noses Are Here and Other Noodle Tales

by Alvin Schwartz
Illustrations by Karen Ann Weinhaus

Noodle tales are silly tales to tell a dog or a best friend. You get five of them in this book.

Just Us Women

by Jeannette Caines
Illustrations by Pat Cummings

A young girl and her aunt take a car trip together and do exactly as they please.

The Sun, the Moon, and the Silver Baboon

Written and illustrated by Susan Field

One night a star comes loose from the sky! Find out how all the animals try to help.

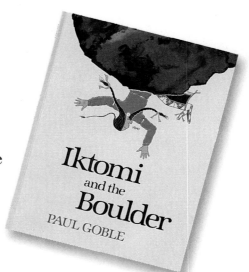

Iktomi and the Boulder

Retold and illustrated by Paul Goble

Iktomi loves to play tricks. But when he tricks a boulder, the boulder gets mad. What will Iktomi do next?

118

Bad Egg: The True Story of Humpty Dumpty

by Sarah Hayes
Illustrations by Charlotte Voake

You know the story of Humpty Dumpty, don't you? Are you sure? You might be surprised by what happens in this story.

Feathers Like a Rainbow: An Amazon Indian Tale

Written and illustrated by Flora

Birds of the jungle have feathers in such beautiful colors. Why? This legend will tell you.

Time to Get Out

Written and illustrated by Fulvio Testa

Captain Nick tells a story of adventure with strange noises and crocodiles. You might be surprised about how he gets the story.

119

Literary Terms

Author

An **author** is a person who writes stories. James Marshall wrote *Three Up a Tree*, so he is the author of that story. When *you* write a story, *you* are the author.

Characters

The people or animals in a story are the **characters**. Rosa and Blanca are two characters you have read about. Who are your favorite characters in this book?

Folk Tales

Folk tales are stories people have told to each other over and over. Folk tales can be about people like Rosa and Blanca. They can also be about animals like Hippo. You may know other folk tales, such as *The Three Little Pigs*.

Illustration

An **illustration** is a picture that goes with a story or poem. Illustrations help tell what happens in a story. They can be drawings, paintings, or photographs.

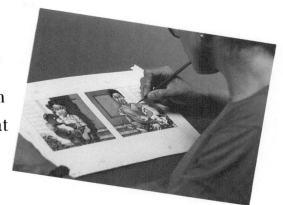

Illustrator

An **illustrator** makes the pictures for a story. When you make your own pictures for a story, you are an illustrator.

Setting

The **setting** is when and where a story happens. Sometimes the pictures in a story show you the setting. *There's a Hole in the Bucket* happens on a farm. You can see the barn, the fields, and the farmyard.

Title

A **title** is the name of a story. *Jimmy Lee Did It* is the title of one story you have read.

JIMMY LEE DID IT

Glossary

Words from your stories

ax

bank

agree   to have the same idea about something: *We all agree that it is a good story.* **agreed, agreeing.**

ax   a tool with a flat, sharp blade used for chopping: *We used an ax to chop wood for the fire.* **axes.** Also spelled **axe.**

bank   **1.** the ground along a river or lake: *He fished from the river bank.* **2.** a place for keeping money: *Mom and Dad put money in the bank every week.* **banks.**

blame   responsibility for something bad or wrong: *Horace took the blame for his brother's mistake.* **blamed, blaming.**

capture   to take by force and hold: *The police will try to capture the robber.* **captured, capturing.**

chile   a hot, spicy pepper used to season food: *I drank a lot of water after biting into a hot chile.* **chiles.** Also **chili, chilies.**

chiles

clever   smart; quick at learning and understanding: *My clever friend won a math contest.* **cleverer, cleverest.**

clue   something that helps find an answer to a question or puzzle: *Give me a clue so I can answer the riddle.* **clues.**

corn   a vegetable that grows on a tall, green plant. It is usually yellow or white. Farm animals and people eat corn: *Jamie picked ten ears of corn for dinner.*

corn

describe   to tell in words how someone or something looks, feels, or acts: *Please describe the giant in the story.* **described, describing.**

dull   not sharp or pointed: *Her dull scissors will not cut the cardboard.* **duller, dullest.**

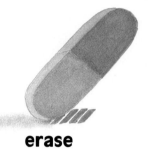

erase

erase   to rub out; wipe out: *He erased his wrong answer and wrote in the right one.* **erased, erasing.**

exactly   without any change; just the right way: *He followed my directions exactly. He looks exactly like his twin.*

final   at the end; coming last: *December 31 is the final day of the year.*

gaze   to look at for a long time: *We gazed at the sunset.* **gazed, gazing.**

half

half   one of two equal parts: *He ate half of an apple for lunch. He had the other half after school. Both halves tasted good.* **halves.**

hopefully   in a hopeful way; showing hope or expecting to get what one wants: *The child looked hopefully toward the door where her mother would come in.*

hungry feeling a need to eat: *She didn't eat breakfast and was hungry all morning.* **hungrier, hungriest.**

imaginary make-believe or made-up; taking place only in the mind: *My brother has an imaginary friend named Pluto.*

listen to try to hear something or someone: *We listened to her story.* **listened, listening.**

monster a make-believe person or animal that is scary. In stories, some monsters are friendly, and others are not: *The children tried to trick the monster.* **monsters.**

monster

mountain a very high hill: *It took them three weeks to climb the mountain.* **mountains.**

mystery something that you cannot understand nor explain: *It was a mystery why the radio started playing in the middle of the night.* **mysteries.**

mountain

photograph

sharp

pass to go by; move past: *The truck passed two cars. Months pass slowly.* **passed, passing.**

photograph a picture you make with a camera: *Will you take a photograph of Wendell and me?* **photographs.**

remain to be left: *A few leaves remain on the tree.* **remained, remaining.**

sharp **1.** with a thin edge or a fine point: *Be careful with that sharp knife. My dog has sharp teeth.* **sharper, sharpest.**

sharpen to make sharp: *The woodsman sharpened his knife on a stone.* **sharpened, sharpening.** See **sharp.**

sketch **1.** to make a quick drawing of something: *Marcy sketched the horse as they drove by the farm.* **2.** a rough, quickly done drawing or design: *Joe made a sketch of the river and hills.* **sketched, sketching; sketches.**

snooze   a nap: *The dog took a snooze in the shade.* **snoozed, snoozing; snoozes.**

straw   the stalks or stems of grain. Straw can be used for animal beds and weaving: *The farmer brought a bunch of straw into the barn for the horses.*

straw

swell   excellent; very nice: *That was a swell movie we saw last week.*

tomato   a round, red fruit. Tomatoes are juicy and grow on vines: *Mike cut up a tomato to put in the salad.* **tomatoes.**

tomato

tortilla   a thin, flat cake, usually made of corn meal or flour and eaten hot. A tortilla is often filled with cheese or meat: *They liked to eat beans and warm tortillas for lunch.* **tortillas.**

tortillas

trace   **1.** to copy by following letters or lines with a pen or pencil: *She traced the picture of the clown.* **2.** a mark or sign that a person or animal has been in a place: *The thief left no trace to help the police find him.* **traced, tracing; traces.**

Acknowledgments

Text

Page 6: From *Three Up a Tree* by James Marshall. Copyright © 1986 by James Marshall. Used by permission of Dial Books for Young Readers, a division of Penguin Books USA Inc.

Page 32: Text and illustrations from *There's a Hole in the Bucket* by Nadine Bernard Westcott. Copyright © 1990 by Nadine Bernard Westcott. Reprinted by permission of HarperCollins Publishers.

Page 52: "On the top of a mountain" and "There's a cow on the mountain" reprinted by permission of Philomel Books from *Chinese Mother Goose Rhymes,* text copyright © 1968 by Robert Wyndham, illustrations copyright © 1968 by Ed Young.

Page 54: "Crickets Are More Than Bugs!" by Ed Young. Copyright © by Ed Young, 1991.

Page 56: *Jimmy Lee Did It* by Pat Cummings. Copyright © 1985 by Pat Cummings. Published by Lothrop, Lee & Shepard Books, a Division of William Morrow & Company, Inc. Publishers.

Page 74: *About Jimmy Lee* by Pat Cummings. Copyright © by Pat Cummings, 1991.

Page 84: "Keep a Poem in Your Pocket" by Beatrice Schenk de Regniers. From *Something Special* by Beatrice Schenk de Regniers. Copyright © 1958 © renewed 1986 by Beatrice Schenk de Regniers. Used by permission of Marian Reiner for the author.

Page 86: *Hot Hippo* by Mwenye Hadithi and Adrienne Kennaway. Copyright © 1986 by Bruce Hobson and Adrienne Kennaway. By permission of Little, Brown and Company.

Page 104: *Rosa and Blanca* by Joe Hayes. Copyright © by Joe Hayes, 1991.

Page 114: "The Gift of a Story" by Joe Hayes. Copyright © by Joe Hayes, 1991.

Artists

Illustrations owned and copyrighted by the illustrator.
Etienne Delessert, cover, 1–3, 117, 122–127
James Marshall, 6–31
Nadine Bernard Westcott, 4, 32–51
Ed Young, 52–55
Pat Cummings, 56–85
Adrienne Kennaway, 5, 86–103
José Ortega, 5, 104–113, 120

Photographs

Unless otherwise acknowledged, all photographs are the property of Scott Foresman.
Page 55: Courtesy of Ed Young
Pages 74–82, 121: Courtesy of Pat Cummings
Pages 5, 114–116: Photos by Oscar Perez, *Casa Grande Dispatch*

Glossary

The contents of this glossary have been adapted from *My Second Picture Dictionary,* Copyright © 1990 Scott, Foresman and Company and *Beginning Dictionary,* Copyright © 1988 Scott, Foresman and Company.